Permission Slips

Shattering Your Perceived Limitations on How Life Should Be

Mary Vernal

Michelle,
You do have a choice. Choose love,
what feels like freedom!!
Love + Light,
Mary Vernal

Dedication

This book is dedicated to all the people over my lifetime who told me, "Shhhh, you're too loud," or criticized my hair, my clothes, my thoughts, my being by rolling their eyes or talking behind my back. It was through the pain you inflicted that I was able to grow and learn to embrace, love, and accept myself fully. That is the greatest gift one can receive. Thank you for that, truly.

It is also dedicated to my biggest supporters, some blood family, others chosen family, who saw me and loved me for who I am, who supported me in the best and worst of times, who held the vision I had for myself when I was unable to. You called me on my shit when necessary and reminded me of who I was and what I was capable of when I started to forget. You are my Tribe. Without you, I couldn't have made it to where I am and that's a damn good place!!

And to my amazing children, Chris and Melanie. Being a guardian for you through your younger years has been the most rewarding work of my life. May you always remember to follow your inner knowing and listen to the whispers of your Soul over your head, even when it makes no logical sense or seems impossible. You are the most magical of beings and I will always love you, no matter what. Thank you for choosing me to be your mother.

Introduction

It took me a long time to understand that I didn't have to live my life based on other people's expectations and what they thought my life should look like. For years I put other people's needs before mine, trying to fulfill all my responsibilities as a wife, mother, daughter, business owner, household manager and family financial officer. My own health and wellbeing weren't even on my to do list. But everything changed the first Thanksgiving after my divorce. I usually hosted the elders, a few siblings, and some strays every year. But with my family broken and my ex and his parents not talking to me, I was torn. I didn't feel like hosting anyone that year, but I was afraid of letting everyone down. As a Spiritual Life Coach, I had many tools at my disposal to work through it all. I remembered what I'd learned in my first life coach training—I had to live it to give it.

So, when I found out my ex and his girlfriend were going to host dinner with his parents and my kids were good with going there, I decided to choose what served me instead. I booked a room at a beautiful inn on the water with a spa for Thanksgiving night. I left early Thursday morning and arrived for an amazing massage. I checked in to a beautiful room with a water view and sat down with my laptop and started to write. I wrote reflections. I wrote hopes and dreams. I wrote brain dumps. I thought about how different this Thanksgiving was, in a good way, and how this was something I never would have done before. I felt so free. I felt so nurtured. I could finally breathe. That's when the inspiration for *Daily Permission Slips* came to be. I created 31 of them as a social media gift to my peeps. It was a gift from my heart to those who were also struggling, those who didn't even realize they had a choice.

That Thanksgiving was a huge turning point for me. One that took a very windy, hard road to get to. The next year, I returned with a determination to create a book with 365 Permission Slips to help people explore other areas that they may need to give themselves permission to change. The result is what you hold in your hands.

This book is to help you understand your life is your own. That you do have choices. Your fate is in your hands. No matter what anybody tells you, you deserve to live a life that is true to your desires, your values, and your dreams. Only you can know what those are. So, today, right now, stop living up to everyone else's expectations. Start giving yourself permission to live the life of your dreams from the smallest choices to the biggest ones, by letting go of that which doesn't fill you with joy and love.

I hope this book will help you decide what you really want your life to look like, and start you on your path to creating a life that is truly yours. You are so worth it!

How To Use This Book

Any way you would like to!!! Some people like to start at the beginning and read a page a day in order. Some people like to "randomly" open to a page every day as a way to be guided to what they most need to hear. Read it backward! This is your reflection and your choice. If you come to a Permission Slip that doesn't resonate with you, that's okay. Just take it in and let it be. Allow yourself to be open to infinite possibilities. My highest hope for this book and for you is that it awakens you to think bigger than you ever have and to take steps to live life on your terms. Go do you, Darling. Only you can. I am here to support you and cheer you on.

Permission Slip

I give myself permission to:

CELEBRATE THAT I'M ALIVE

1

Permission Slip

I give myself permission to:

BE MY OWN
BEST FRIEND

Permission Slip

I give myself permission to:

SEND LOVE
TO MY BODY

Permission Slip

I give myself permission to:

SAY NO
TO TRADITIONS

Permission Slip

I give myself permission to:

APPRECIATE THE LITTLE THINGS

Permission Slip

I give myself permission to:

BE MY
OWN HERO

Permission Slip

I give myself permission to:

AGE GRACEFULLY

Permission Slip

I give myself permission to:

BUY THE SHOES

Permission Slip

I give myself permission to:

DECIDE WHAT LOVE LOOKS LIKE

Permission Slip

I give myself permission to:

EAT WHATEVER
I WANT

Permission Slip

I give myself permission to:

ASTOUND PEOPLE

Permission Slip

I give myself permission to:

DECIDE

YES OR NO

Permission Slip

I give myself permission to:

MAKE A FOOL OF MYSELF

Permission Slip

I give myself permission to:

CHOOSE WHO IS ALLOWED IN MY HOME

Permission Slip

I give myself permission to:

WEAR A BIKINI

Permission Slip

I give myself permission to:

STOP DOING WHAT'S EXPECTED OF ME

Permission Slip

I give myself permission to:

TAKE A
LONG WALK
IN THE WOODS

Permission Slip

I give myself permission to:

GO BACK TO SCHOOL

Permission Slip

I give myself permission to:

EXPRESS MY SEXUALITY HOWEVER I WANT

Permission Slip

I give myself permission to:

BE A REBEL

Permission Slip

I give myself permission to:

CALL MEAN GIRLS OUT

Permission Slip

I give myself permission to:

CELEBRATE EACH LITTLE THING

Permission Slip

I give myself permission to:

FEEL THE WIND IN MY HAIR

Permission Slip

I give myself permission to:

DECIDE HOW
I WANT TO LIVE
MY LIFE

Permission Slip

I give myself permission to:

NEVER STOP TRYING

Permission Slip

I give myself permission to:

RETHINK SOMETHING

Permission Slip

I give myself permission to:

STOP AND
BREATHE

Permission Slip

I give myself permission to:

OVERLOOK THE SMALL TRANSGRESSIONS

Permission Slip

I give myself permission to:

MAKE OTHER PEOPLE RESPONSIBLE FOR THEIR OWN LIVES

29

Permission Slip

I give myself permission to:

STOP DOING WHAT I'VE ALWAYS DONE

Permission Slip

I give myself permission to:

WONDER WHY

Permission Slip

I give myself permission to:

STOP JUDGING MYSELF

Permission Slip

I give myself permission to:

SET BOUNDARIES

Permission Slip

I give myself permission to:

PAMPER MYSELF

Permission Slip

I give myself permission to:

LIVE MY LIFE MY WAY

Permission Slip

I give myself permission to:

GET OUT
OF A RELATIONSHIP

Permission Slip

I give myself permission to:

BE IN AWE
OF THE SUNRISE

Permission Slip

I give myself permission to:

CONTEMPLATE THE MEANING OF LIFE

Permission Slip

I give myself permission to:

BE LOUD

Permission Slip

I give myself permission to:

ACCEPT

MY MISTAKES

Permission Slip

I give myself permission to:

Celebrate my body and all it can do

Permission Slip

I give myself permission to:

DO BIG THINGS
IN THE WORLD

Permission Slip

I give myself permission to:

STOP AND LISTEN TO THE BIRDS

Permission Slip

I give myself permission to:

BE ADVENTUROUS

Permission Slip

I give myself permission to:

CELEBRATE
FOR NO REASON

Permission Slip

I give myself permission to:

DECIDE WHAT
MAKES ME HAPPY

Permission Slip

I give myself permission to:

FIND AT LEAST
ONE MIRACLE A DAY

Permission Slip

I give myself permission to:

KEEP TRYING
NEW THINGS

Permission Slip

I give myself permission to:

NOT BACK DOWN

Permission Slip

I give myself permission to:

RUFFLE FEATHERS

Permission Slip

I give myself permission to:

TREAT MY BODY
AS A MIRACLE

Permission Slip

I give myself permission to:

TRAVEL ALONE

Permission Slip

I give myself permission to:

NOT ANSWER SOMEONE'S QUESTIONS

Permission Slip

I give myself permission to:

SING AT THE TOP OF MY LUNGS

Permission Slip

I give myself permission to:

WANT MORE

Permission Slip

I give myself permission to:

STOP HIDING

Permission Slip

I give myself permission to:

Seek

UNDERSTANDING

Permission Slip

I give myself permission to:

PAINT MY WALLS
ANY COLOR
I WANT

Permission Slip

I give myself permission to:

LIVE BIG

Permission Slip

I give myself permission to:

GET IT WRONG

Permission Slip

I give myself permission to:

DRESS ANY WAY THAT MAKES ME FEEL GREAT

Permission Slip

I give myself permission to:

CLOSE MY EYES
AND LISTEN
TO THE RUNNING
WATER

Permission Slip

I give myself permission to:

DO LIFE MY WAY

Permission Slip

I give myself permission to:

ACCEPT

MY LIMITATIONS

Permission Slip

I give myself permission to:

CELEBRATE HOW AMAZING AND MIRACULOUS MY BODY IS

Permission Slip

I give myself permission to:

DYE MY HAIR

Permission Slip

I give myself permission to:

TAKE EXCELLENT CARE OF MYSELF

Permission Slip

I give myself permission to:

ASK QUESTIONS

Permission Slip

I give myself permission to:

BUILD A

SANDCASTLE

Permission Slip

I give myself permission to:

DECIDE WHAT
I'M WILLING TO PUT
UP WITH

70

Permission Slip

I give myself permission to:

FAIL

Permission Slip

I give myself permission to:

HAVE TOUGH
CONVERSATIONS

Permission Slip

I give myself permission to:

RELOCATE

Permission Slip

I give myself permission to:

STAY SINGLE

Permission Slip

I give myself permission to:

TAKE TIME TO FEEL THE SUN ON MY FACE

Permission Slip

I give myself permission to:

BE IN AWE
OF MY BODY
EVERY DAY

Permission Slip

I give myself permission to:

SET MY OWN

SCHEDULE

Permission Slip

I give myself permission to:

WALK AWAY FROM ANYONE FOR MY OWN HEALTH

78

Permission Slip

I give myself permission to:

STOP GOSSIP
WHEN I HEAR IT

Permission Slip

I give myself permission to:

SEEK THE HELP
I NEED

Permission Slip

I give myself permission to:

TOTALLY CHANGE MY LIFE

Permission Slip

I give myself permission to:

LET THAT SHIT GO

Permission Slip

I give myself permission to:

GET BETTER
WITH AGE

Permission Slip

I give myself permission to:

DISREGARD ASSHOLES

Permission Slip

I give myself permission to:

CLOSE MY EYES
AND LISTEN
TO THE WAVES

85

Permission Slip

I give myself permission to:

BE IN AWE
OF LIFE

Permission Slip

I give myself permission to:

ACCEPT MY FAULTS

Permission Slip

I give myself permission to:

LET GO OF OTHER PEOPLE'S EXPECTATIONS

Permission Slip

I give myself permission to:

LOVE MY BODY EXACTLY AS IT IS

Permission Slip

I give myself permission to:

ADMIT
I WAS WRONG

Permission Slip

I give myself permission to:

BE SASSY

Permission Slip

I give myself permission to:

DATE MYSELF

Permission Slip

I give myself permission to:

EMBRACE
MY IMPERFECTIONS

Permission Slip

I give myself permission to:

MOVE AS OFTEN AS I WISH

Permission Slip

I give myself permission to:

GO FLY A KITE

Permission Slip

I give myself permission to:

PUSH
THE BOUNDARIES

Permission Slip

I give myself permission to:

SPEAK UP FOR SOMEONE

Permission Slip

I give myself permission to:

TAKE A LONG WALK
ON THE BEACH

Permission Slip

I give myself permission to:

DANCE IN THE GROCERY STORE

Permission Slip

I give myself permission to:

SAY NO TO ANYONE, ANYTIME FOR WHATEVER REASON

100

Permission Slip

I give myself permission to:

ENJOY AND CELEBRATE MY NAKED BODY

Permission Slip

I give myself permission to:

PUSH BACK

Permission Slip

I give myself permission to:

CELEBRATE

THE MIRACLE

OF ME

Permission Slip

I give myself permission to:

DO SOMETHING I'VE NEVER DONE BEFORE

Permission Slip

I give myself permission to:

GROW

Permission Slip

I give myself permission to:

NOT CONFORM

Permission Slip

I give myself permission to:

SEEK KNOWLEDGE

Permission Slip

I give myself permission to:

TAKE A LONG, HOT BATH

Permission Slip

I give myself permission to:

LET SOMEONE ELSE DO THE COOKING

Permission Slip

I give myself permission to:

SAY HELL NO TO WHAT "SOCIETY" SAYS I MUST DO

Permission Slip

I give myself permission to:

TRY AGAIN

Permission Slip

I give myself permission to:

STAY IN ONE PLACE

Permission Slip

I give myself permission to:

APPRECIATE
MY BODY
EXACTLY HOW IT IS

Permission Slip

I give myself permission to:

LET PEOPLE GO

Permission Slip

I give myself permission to:

FIND JOY
IN EVERY DAY

Permission Slip

I give myself permission to:

DECIDE FOR MYSELF

Permission Slip

I give myself permission to:

BE HONEST

Permission Slip

I give myself permission to:

Workout however my body wants me to

Permission Slip

I give myself permission to:

GO BRALESS

Permission Slip

I give myself permission to:

LEAVE A RELATIONSHIP THAT DOESN'T FULFILL ME

Permission Slip

I give myself permission to:

GO AFTER
WHAT I WANT

Permission Slip

I give myself permission to:

NOT BE IN STYLE

Permission Slip

I give myself permission to:

SHAKE THINGS UP

Permission Slip

I give myself permission to:

ACCEPT OTHER PEOPLE'S LIMITATIONS

Permission Slip

I give myself permission to:

STAY UP ALL NIGHT

Permission Slip

I give myself permission to:

PURSUE MY OWN HEALING

Permission Slip

I give myself permission to:

STAND UP FOR SOMEONE BEING BULLIED

Permission Slip

I give myself permission to:

TREAT MYSELF LAVISHLY

Permission Slip

I give myself permission to:

REJECT SOMEONE'S ADVANCES

Permission Slip

I give myself permission to:

TAKE TIME FOR MYSELF

Permission Slip

I give myself permission to:

WEAR WHAT
I WANT WHEREVER
I WANT

Permission Slip

I give myself permission to:

APPRECIATE
MY LIFE
EXACTLY HOW IT IS

132

Permission Slip

I give myself permission to:

CHANGE MY MIND

Permission Slip

I give myself permission to:

END A FRIENDSHIP NO MATTER HOW LONG IT'S BEEN

134

Permission Slip

I give myself permission to:

STOP MAKING
IT MY JOB
TO FIX THINGS

135

Permission Slip

I give myself permission to:

PURSUE MY DREAMS

Permission Slip

I give myself permission to:

STOP AND WATCH A WORM MOVE

Permission Slip

I give myself permission to:

DANCE ALL NIGHT

Permission Slip

I give myself permission to:

REFUSE
TO BE TOUCHED

Permission Slip

I give myself permission to:

LET MY HAIR
BE A MESS

Permission Slip

I give myself permission to:

BE BETTER

Permission Slip

I give myself permission to:

ASK FOR WHAT I WANT IN A SEXUAL RELATIONSHIP

142

Permission Slip

I give myself permission to:

CREATE A HOME
THAT I LOVE

Permission Slip

I give myself permission to:

EXPECT OPEN COMMUNICATION

Permission Slip

I give myself permission to:

LIVE THE LIFE
OF MY DREAMS

Permission Slip

I give myself permission to:

REJECT OTHER PEOPLE'S OPINIONS

Permission Slip

I give myself permission to:

STOP PLAYING SMALL

Permission Slip

I give myself permission to:

NOT HUG SOMEONE

Permission Slip

I give myself permission to:

TREAT MY FRIENDS LAVISHLY

Permission Slip

I give myself permission to:

LET MY HAIR
BE GRAY

Permission Slip

I give myself permission to:

ACCEPT REALITY

Permission Slip

I give myself permission to:

CHANGE AND CHANGE AGAIN

Permission Slip

I give myself permission to:

ENJOY BEING ALONE

Permission Slip

I give myself permission to:

LET GO
OF THE PAST

Permission Slip

I give myself permission to:

RECOGNIZE
I'M A WORK
IN PROGRESS

155

Permission Slip

I give myself permission to:

STOP JUDGING
OTHER PEOPLE

Permission Slip

I give myself permission to:

Outsource Anything

Permission Slip

I give myself permission to:

TRY A NEW KIND OF FOOD

Permission Slip

I give myself permission to:

SHUT DOWN
THE MEAN GIRLS

Permission Slip

I give myself permission to:

MAKE THE WORLD
A BETTER PLACE

Permission Slip

I give myself permission to:

FUCK UP

Permission Slip

I give myself permission to:

DECIDE IF SOMETHING IS RIGHT FOR ME

Permission Slip

I give myself permission to:

BE FIRM

Permission Slip

I give myself permission to:

PROTECT MY BODY

Permission Slip

I give myself permission to:

SLEEP NAKED

Permission Slip

I give myself permission to:

ADJUST MY

WORKOUT FOR WHAT

I NEED TODAY

Permission Slip

I give myself permission to:

ASK FOR
WHAT I WANT

Permission Slip

I give myself permission to:

DECIDE WHO
I WANT TO SPEND
MY TIME WITH

Permission Slip

I give myself permission to:

FORGIVE FOR MY OWN HEALING AND NO ONE ELSE'S

169

Permission Slip

I give myself permission to:

MEET NEW PEOPLE

Permission Slip

I give myself permission to:

SPEAK MY TRUTH

Permission Slip

I give myself permission to:

BE WHO I AM, UNAPOLOGETICALLY

Permission Slip

I give myself permission to:

REFUSE TO ACCEPT MEDIOCRITY

Permission Slip

I give myself permission to:

TAKE CHARGE
OF MY HEALTH

Permission Slip

I give myself permission to:

RUN AWAY FOR A BIT

Permission Slip

I give myself permission to:

LET GO OF WHAT
I THOUGHT
I WANTED

Permission Slip

I give myself permission to:

EMBRACE MY AGE

Permission Slip

I give myself permission to:

BUCK
THE STATUS QUO

Permission Slip

I give myself permission to:

STOP MAKING EXCUSES FOR OTHER PEOPLE

Permission Slip

I give myself permission to:

STOP SHAVING

Permission Slip

I give myself permission to:

LOVE MY ROLLS

Permission Slip

I give myself permission to:

BE QUIET

Permission Slip

I give myself permission to:

DECIDE WHO
I WANT TO
CONFIDE IN

Permission Slip

I give myself permission to:

JOIN A GYM

Permission Slip

I give myself permission to:

BE SAPPY

Permission Slip

I give myself permission to:

TAKE A DAY OFF

186

Permission Slip

I give myself permission to:

NOT KISS SOMEONE

Permission Slip

I give myself permission to:

WALK AWAY FROM ABUSE

Permission Slip

I give myself permission to:

SEE THINGS IN A NEW WAY

189

Permission Slip

I give myself permission to:

LOVE PEOPLE ANYWAY

Permission Slip

I give myself permission to:

EXPECT MORE
THAN MEDIOCRITY

Permission Slip

I give myself permission to:

BUY MYSELF
FLOWERS

Permission Slip

I give myself permission to:

MAKE WHATEVER DECISIONS ARE BEST FOR MY FAMILY

Permission Slip

I give myself permission to:

UPGRADE
MY LINGERIE

Permission Slip

I give myself permission to:

REST

Permission Slip

I give myself permission to:

BE TENACIOUS

196

Permission Slip

I give myself permission to:

DO WHAT I WANT

Permission Slip

I give myself permission to:

LOOK SILLY

Permission Slip

I give myself permission to:

SEE THE TRUTH

Permission Slip

I give myself permission to:

BE AFFECTIONATE IN PUBLIC

Permission Slip

I give myself permission to:

NOT BE POLITICALLY CORRECT

Permission Slip

I give myself permission to:

LOVE MY LINES

Permission Slip

I give myself permission to:

QUIT THE GYM

Permission Slip

I give myself permission to:

DREAM BIG

Permission Slip

I give myself permission to:

LOVE MYSELF FULLY

Permission Slip

I give myself permission to:

SIT AND WATCH THE SUNSET

Permission Slip

I give myself permission to:

HIRE HELP

Permission Slip

I give myself permission to:

TAKE TIME
TO STARE
AT THE STARS

Permission Slip

I give myself permission to:

RELEASE WHAT NO LONGER SERVES ME

Permission Slip

I give myself permission to:

HAVE AS MANY KIDS AS I WANT, EVEN ZERO

Permission Slip

I give myself permission to:

Decide what is no longer tolerable

Permission Slip

I give myself permission to:

BE BIG

Permission Slip

I give myself permission to:

WEAR BRIGHT COLORS THAT MAKE ME HAPPY

Permission Slip

I give myself permission to:

SEE WHAT MY BODY IS CAPABLE OF

Permission Slip

I give myself permission to:

BE WHO I AM WITH NO EXCUSES

Permission Slip

I give myself permission to:

FEEL HOW I FEEL

Permission Slip

I give myself permission to:

NOT ENGAGE
WITH MEAN GIRLS

Permission Slip

I give myself permission to:

STOP BEING
AVAILABLE
TO TOXIC PEOPLE

218

Permission Slip

I give myself permission to:

HAVE BREAKFAST FOR DINNER

Permission Slip

I give myself permission to:

Take

responsibility

for my own life

Permission Slip

I give myself permission to:

PURSUE MY OWN INTERESTS

Permission Slip

I give myself permission to:

GIVE ZERO FUCKS

Permission Slip

I give myself permission to:

CREATE SOMETHING NEW IN THE KITCHEN

Permission Slip

I give myself permission to:

Accept myself
for who I am

Permission Slip

I give myself permission to:

WEAR FABRIC NEXT TO MY SKIN THAT FEELS INCREDIBLE

225

Permission Slip

I give myself permission to:

TAKE A LONG, LUXURIOUS BATH

Permission Slip

I give myself permission to:

CELEBRATE

MY UNIQUENESS

Permission Slip

I give myself permission to:

FORGIVE BUT NOT CONDONE

228

Permission Slip

I give myself permission to:

PRACTICE EXTREME SELF-LOVE

Permission Slip

I give myself permission to:

TAKE MYSELF OUT TO A NICE DINNER

Permission Slip

I give myself permission to:

GO AGAINST
THE GRAIN

Permission Slip

I give myself permission to:

STARE AT THE OCEAN AS LONG AS I WANT

Permission Slip

I give myself permission to:

LOVE FROM
A DISTANCE

Permission Slip

I give myself permission to:

DECIDE WHO
GETS ACCESS TO ME

234

Permission Slip

I give myself permission to:

BE AFRAID AND
DO IT ANYWAY

235

Permission Slip

I give myself permission to:

GIVE UP
THE WORKOUTS
THAT MAKE
MY BODY HURT

Permission Slip

I give myself permission to:

ACCEPT

MY SHORTCOMINGS

237

Permission Slip

I give myself permission to:

DECIDE HOW
I WANT
MY DAYS TO BE

Permission Slip

I give myself permission to:

LEARN
HOW TO FIX IT
MYSELF

Permission Slip

I give myself permission to:

SLEEP TIL NOON

Permission Slip

I give myself permission to:

EAT DESSERT FIRST

Permission Slip

I give myself permission to:

STOP, JUST STOP

Permission Slip

I give myself permission to:

NOT SETTLE

Permission Slip

I give myself permission to:

EXPECT HONESTY

Permission Slip

I give myself permission to:

BE ME

Permission Slip

I give myself permission to:

GO FOR A WALK
AND LET THAT BE
ENOUGH FOR TODAY

246

Permission Slip

I give myself permission to:

RAISE MY KIDS
MY WAY

247

Permission Slip

I give myself permission to:

DECIDE MAYBE BUT NOT NOW

Permission Slip

I give myself permission to:

LIVE WHERE
I WANT TO LIVE

249

Permission Slip

I give myself permission to:

STOP AND SMELL THE FLOWERS

Permission Slip

I give myself permission to:

DO NOTHING

Permission Slip

I give myself permission to:

Take a new job

Permission Slip

I give myself permission to:

NOT KNOW ALL THE ANSWERS

253

Permission Slip

I give myself permission to:

ASK PEOPLE TO LEAVE

Permission Slip

I give myself permission to:

HAVE CONSENSUAL SEX WITH WHOMEVER I WANT TO

255

Permission Slip

I give myself permission to:

CHANGE THE WORLD

Permission Slip

I give myself permission to:

GO FOR IT

Permission Slip

I give myself permission to:

SEE THE BEAUTY IN EVERY DAY

Permission Slip

I give myself permission to:

DO IT MY WAY

Permission Slip

I give myself permission to:

DISAPPOINT PEOPLE

260

Permission Slip

I give myself permission to:

PROTECT
MY SACRED SPACE

Permission Slip

I give myself permission to:

EXPERIMENT

Permission Slip

I give myself permission to:

BE BRAVE

Permission Slip

I give myself permission to:

BREAK TRADITIONS

Permission Slip

I give myself permission to:

SHOW MY GRATITUDE OPENLY

Permission Slip

I give myself permission to:

GO AFTER

MY DREAMS

Permission Slip

I give myself permission to:

**BEGIN AGAIN,
AND AGAIN**

Permission Slip

I give myself permission to:

LET MY BODY REST

Permission Slip

I give myself permission to:

ACCEPT THE TRUTH

Permission Slip

I give myself permission to:

DELEGATE WHATEVER I WANT TO

Permission Slip

I give myself permission to:

OFFER COMPASSION

Permission Slip

I give myself permission to:

TRAVEL WITH FRIENDS

Permission Slip

I give myself permission to:

REMOVE TOXIC PEOPLE FROM MY LIFE

Permission Slip

I give myself permission to:

FOLLOW MY DREAMS

Permission Slip

I give myself permission to:

BE ON MY OWN

Permission Slip

I give myself permission to:

PLEASURE MYSELF AS OFTEN AS I LIKE

Permission Slip

I give myself permission to:

LET GO OF MY PARENTS' VISION FOR ME

Permission Slip

I give myself permission to:

DO SOMETHING DIFFERENT

Permission Slip

I give myself permission to:

QUIT MY JOB

Permission Slip

I give myself permission to:

CANCEL PLANS

Permission Slip

I give myself permission to:

STRETCH MYSELF

Permission Slip

I give myself permission to:

LET GO OF TRYING
TO CHANGE OTHERS

Permission Slip

I give myself permission to:

CHOOSE
MY OWN PATH

Permission Slip

I give myself permission to:

TAKE A NAP
WHEN I WANT ONE

Permission Slip

I give myself permission to:

CHANGE MY JOB

Permission Slip

I give myself permission to:

DECIDE WHAT

MY DAY

WILL LOOK LIKE

286

Permission Slip

I give myself permission to:

LET GO OF BEATING MYSELF UP FOR PAST MISTAKES

287

Permission Slip

I give myself permission to:

START OVER

Permission Slip

I give myself permission to:

STOP DOING THAT THING I HATE

289

Permission Slip

I give myself permission to:

**BREAK OUT
IN DANCE**

Permission Slip

I give myself permission to:

MAKE MY HOME A REFLECTION OF WHO I AM

291

Permission Slip

I give myself permission to:

CREATE RELATIONSHIPS ANY WAY I WANT THEM TO BE

292

Permission Slip

I give myself permission to:

TRAVEL TO EXOTIC PLACES

293

Permission Slip

I give myself permission to:

ADMIT WHEN
I'M IN OVER
MY HEAD

Permission Slip

I give myself permission to:

BE CURIOUS

Permission Slip

I give myself permission to:

Decide what I want my future to be

Permission Slip

I give myself permission to:

GIVE MYSELF
A BREAK

Permission Slip

I give myself permission to:

MAKE IT HAPPEN

Permission Slip

I give myself permission to:

NEVER GIVE UP

Permission Slip

I give myself permission to:

DANCE BY MYSELF

Permission Slip

I give myself permission to:

EMBARRASS
MY KIDS

Permission Slip

I give myself permission to:

FIND MY JOY

Permission Slip

I give myself permission to:

STAND UP FOR MYSELF

Permission Slip

I give myself permission to:

BE A REBEL

Permission Slip

I give myself permission to:

STOP CRITICIZING MYSELF

Permission Slip

I give myself permission to:

ORDER IN WHENEVER I WANT TO

Permission Slip

I give myself permission to:

EAT LUNCH
BY THE WATER

Permission Slip

I give myself permission to:

HAVE SOME ALONE TIME

Permission Slip

I give myself permission to:

BE DEMANDING

Permission Slip

I give myself permission to:

EXPECT ADULT BEHAVIOR FROM ADULTS

Permission Slip

I give myself permission to:

FLOAT

IN THE WATER

Permission Slip

I give myself permission to:

STAY IN
A RELATIONSHIP

Permission Slip

I give myself permission to:

TRY NEW FORMS OF EXERCISE

Permission Slip

I give myself permission to:

STOP BEATING UP ON MYSELF

Permission Slip

I give myself permission to:

FORGIVE MYSELF

Permission Slip

I give myself permission to:

ACCEPT PEOPLE FOR WHO THEY ARE

Permission Slip

I give myself permission to:

ACCEPT OTHER PEOPLE'S SHORTCOMINGS

Permission Slip

I give myself permission to:

BE VULNERABLE

Permission Slip

I give myself permission to:

MAKE MY OWN TRADITIONS

Permission Slip

I give myself permission to:

THROW AWAY
MY SCALE

Permission Slip

I give myself permission to:

LAUGH AT MYSELF

Permission Slip

I give myself permission to:

BE OUTRAGEOUS

Permission Slip

I give myself permission to:

APPRECIATE
BEING ALIVE

Permission Slip

I give myself permission to:

LOVE WHO I LOVE

Permission Slip

I give myself permission to:

BE UNIQUE

Permission Slip

I give myself permission to:

DESIGN RELATIONSHIPS THAT WORK FOR ME

Permission Slip

I give myself permission to:

SCRAP IT ALL

Permission Slip

I give myself permission to:

TRAVEL THE WORLD

Permission Slip

I give myself permission to:

PRACTICE RADICAL SELF-CARE

329

Permission Slip

I give myself permission to:

STOP CRITICIZING OTHERS

Permission Slip

I give myself permission to:

CHASE WAVES
LIKE A KID

Permission Slip

I give myself permission to:

ASK FOR
FORGIVENESS

Permission Slip

I give myself permission to:

DECORATE ANYWAY I CHOOSE

Permission Slip

I give myself permission to:

BE RESOURCEFUL

Permission Slip

I give myself permission to:

HAVE A
BEGINNER'S MIND

Permission Slip

I give myself permission to:

DECIDE IF *I* SHOULD STAY OR IF *I* SHOULD GO

Permission Slip

I give myself permission to:

ORDER TOPSHELF

Permission Slip

I give myself permission to:

SPEND MY TIME AS I CHOOSE TO

Permission Slip

I give myself permission to:

CREATE A LIFE
THAT FEEDS
MY SOUL

339

Permission Slip

I give myself permission to:

ASK FOR HELP

Permission Slip

I give myself permission to:

GIVE AWAY ANYTHING, NO MATTER WHERE IT CAME FROM

Permission Slip

I give myself permission to:

DANCE WITH
A STRANGER

Permission Slip

I give myself permission to:

SAY "NO"
TO ANYTHING
I DON'T WANT TO DO

343

Permission Slip

I give myself permission to:

MAKE MY OWN RULES

Permission Slip

I give myself permission to:

TAKE TIME TO APPRECIATE THE SKY

Permission Slip

I give myself permission to:

DECIDE WHAT MY PRIORITES ARE

346

Permission Slip

I give myself permission to:

REINVENT MYSELF
AS OFTEN
AS I WISH

347

Permission Slip

I give myself permission to:

BE COURAGEOUS

Permission Slip

I give myself permission to:

PUT MYSELF FIRST

349

Permission Slip

I give myself permission to:

HAVE A LAZY DAY

Permission Slip

I give myself permission to:

STOP SETTLING

Permission Slip

I give myself permission to:

SAY WHAT
I WANT TO SAY

Permission Slip

I give myself permission to:

SET MY OWN BAR

Permission Slip

I give myself permission to:

STOP DOING IT ALL MYSELF

Permission Slip

I give myself permission to:

STOP AND SEE THE BEAUTY AROUND ME

355

Permission Slip

I give myself permission to:

SEE THE BEAUTY IN MY "MISTAKES"

Permission Slip

I give myself permission to:

ONLY KEEP BELONGINGS I LOVE

Permission Slip

I give myself permission to:

GIVE MYSELF WHAT I NEED

Permission Slip

I give myself permission to:

MAKE A SCENE

Permission Slip

I give myself permission to:

LET GO OF CARING
WHAT ANYONE
THINKS OF ME

Permission Slip

I give myself permission to:

DECIDE WHAT SETTLING LOOKS LIKE FOR ME

Permission Slip

I give myself permission to:

ENJOY LIFE

Permission Slip

I give myself permission to:

EXPRESS MYSELF HONESTLY

Permission Slip

I give myself permission to:

BELIEVE WHAT
I BELIEVE

Permission Slip

I give myself permission to:

GO ON A
WILD ADVENTURE

Made in the USA
Middletown, DE
05 June 2019